SCHIRMER'S LIBRARY
OF MUSICAL CLASSICS

Vol. 1804

JOSEPH HAYDN

Trumpet Concerto

For Trumpet and Piano

Piano reduction by
CARL BOWMAN

ISBN 978-0-7935-5195-8

G. SCHIRMER, Inc.

DISTRIBUTED BY

HAL•LEONARD®
CORPORATION

7777 W. BLUEMOUND RD. P.O. BOX 13819 MILWAUKEE, WI 53213

Trumpet Concerto

I

Joseph Haydn
Piano reduction by Carl Bowman

44594Cx

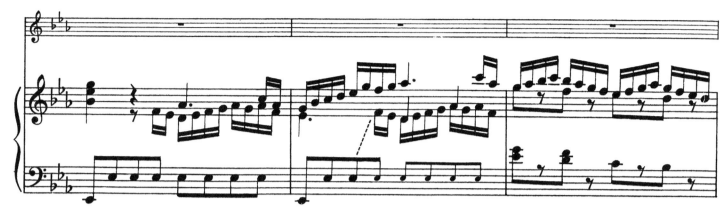

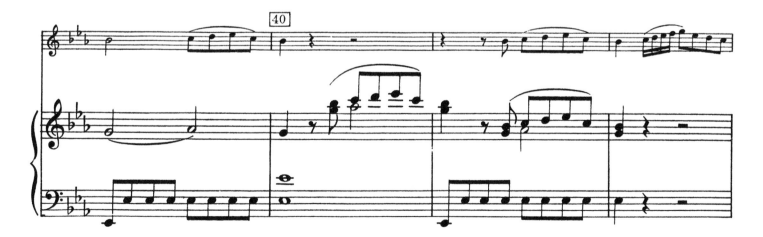

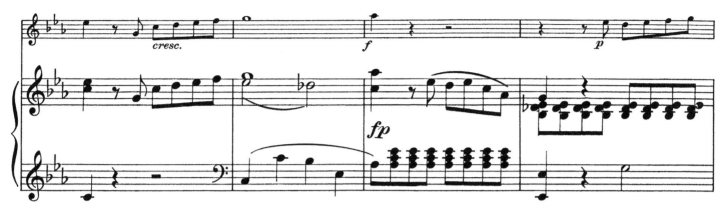

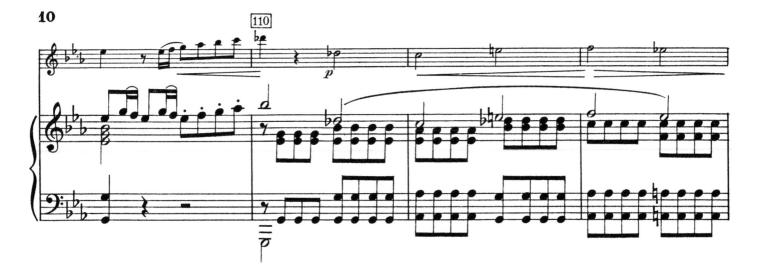

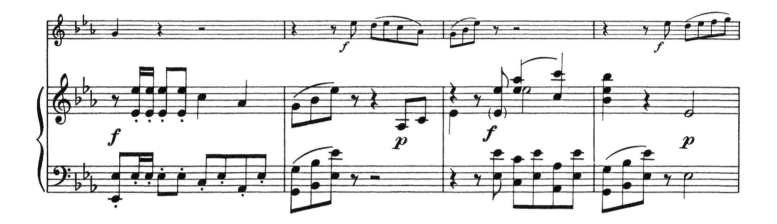

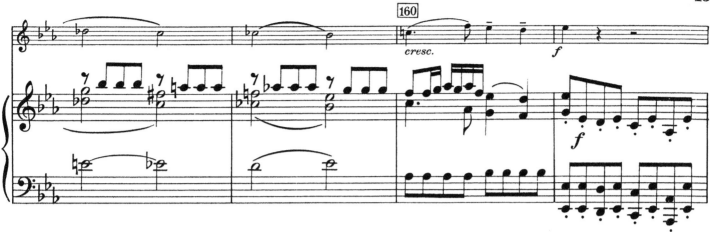

*As far as the editor knows, Haydn wrote no cadenzas for this concerto.

II

Andante

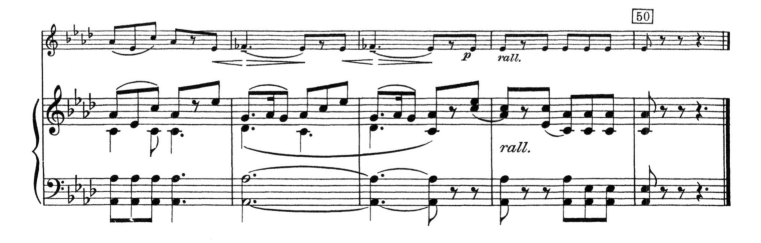

TRUMPET

SCHIRMER'S LIBRARY
OF MUSICAL CLASSICS

Vol. 1804

JOSEPH HAYDN

Trumpet Concerto

For Trumpet and Piano

Piano reduction by
CARL BOWMAN

ISBN 978-0-7935-5195-8

G. SCHIRMER, Inc.

DISTRIBUTED BY

HAL•LEONARD®
CORPORATION
7777 W. BLUEMOUND RD. P.O. BOX 13819 MILWAUKEE, WI 53213

Trumpet Concerto

Trumpet in B♭

Joseph Haydn
Piano reduction by Carl Bowman

I

Trumpet in B♭

*As far as the editor knows, Haydn wrote no cadenzas for this concerto.

II

Trumpet in B♭

III

Allegro

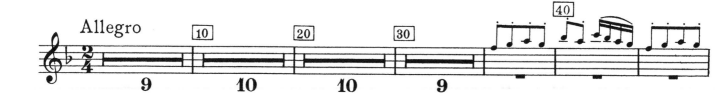

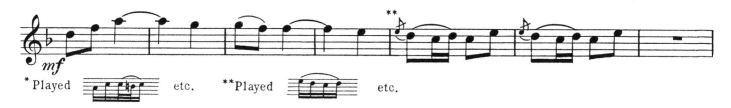

*Played [notation] etc.   **Played [notation] etc.

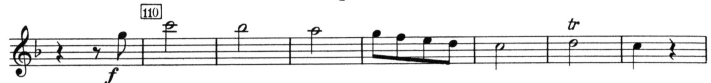

Trumpet in B♭

III

Allegro

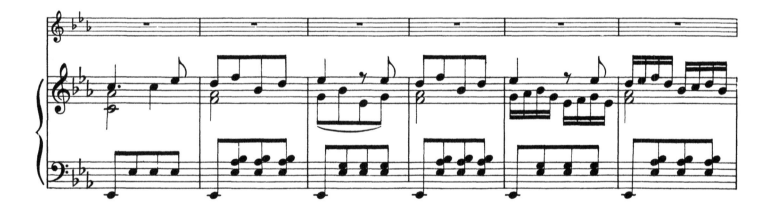

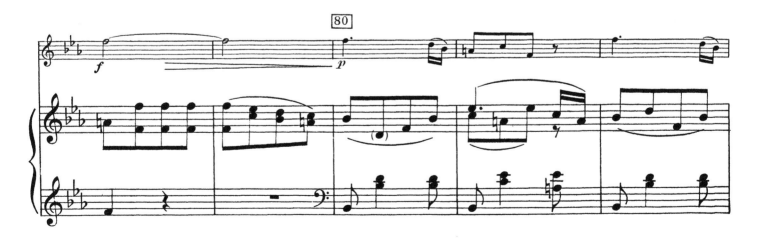

90

100

*Played ♪♪♪♪ etc.

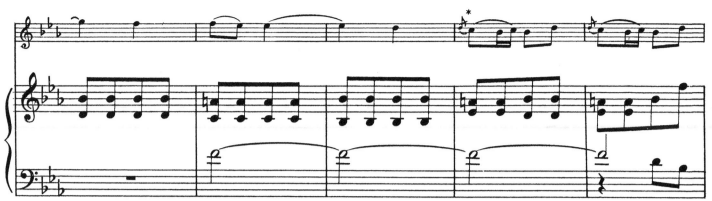

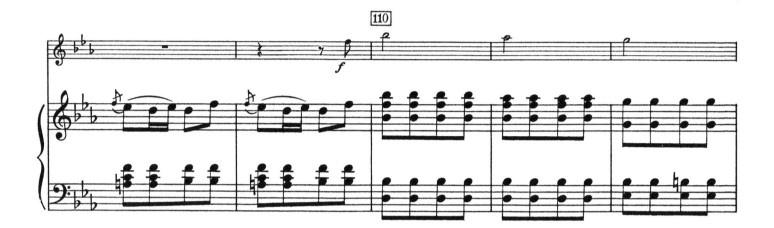

* Played ♪♪♪ etc.

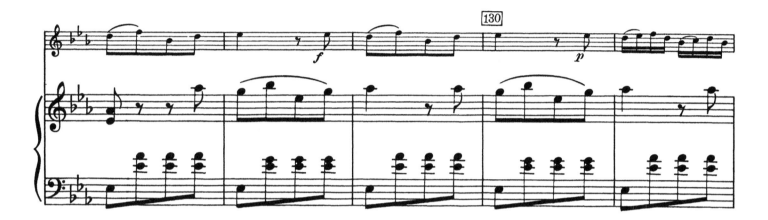

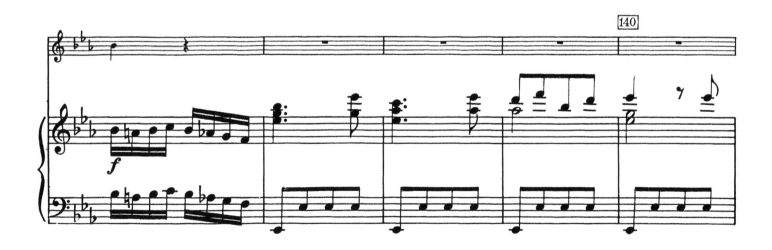

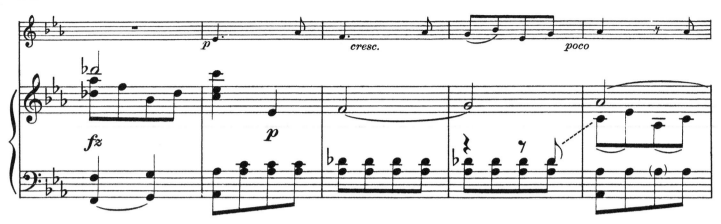

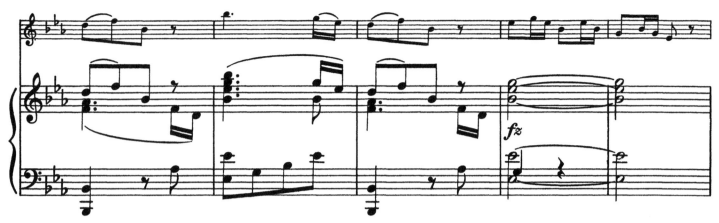

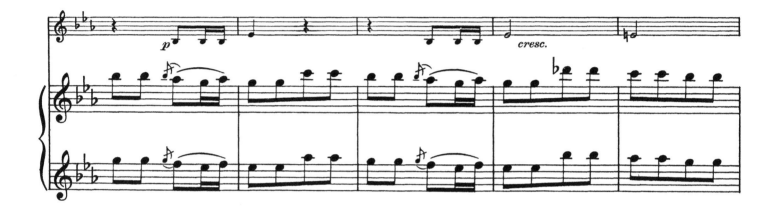

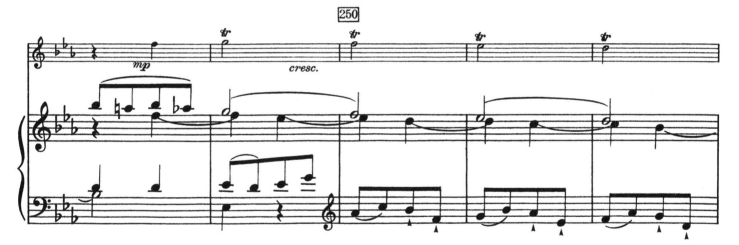

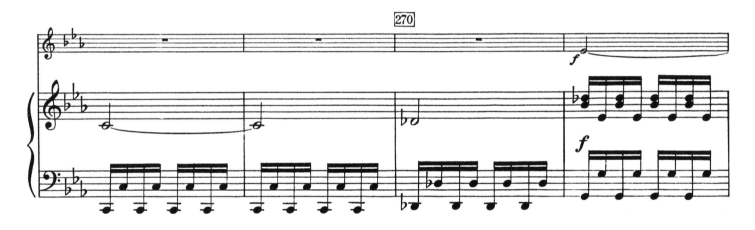

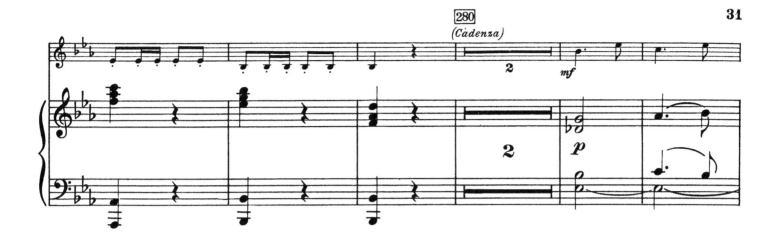